LiStEN to me!

This book has been written to help parents to secure the very best support for their children.

Stand up for what is right and never back down.

Chris
September 2021

Introduction

At the time of writing there are over 1.4 million children recorded as having special educational needs (SEN) in England. This represents over 12% of the school population.

Given what many parents have reported to me from certain schools and local authorities, including a reluctance to place some children on the SEN register, it is considered that this figure is likely to be significantly higher in reality.

Children with SEN are entitled to, from both a moral and a legal perspective, the support that they need to receive a suitable education, to flourish and to achieve their potential.

However, all too often, I hear from parents that securing support for their children is a constant and incredibly stressful battle. When many parents have attempted to ask for assessments of their child, have asked for provisions to be put in place to support them, or have requested an assessment for an EHCP for example, they have simply been met with resistance. Parents have also often stated that they feel as though they are not listened to or not believed. Others feel that certain staff simply say one thing then do another.

Further, many parents have also reported to me that they have been told information that is simply untrue. I find this increasingly shocking. Parents have said to me that they have been told things such as, "teachers do not have to adjust their lesson plans as they don't have time", or "our local authority uses a 30-week process for EHCPs", or that "a child has to be 3-years behind to get an EHCP".

Other parents have reportedly been told that if their child is unable to attend school due to ill-health, that "neither the school nor the local authority have to provide any education". These statements are unacceptable - the rights of every child are embedded in law.

It is sad and disappointing to hear that parents face such struggles, especially when the laws relating to SEN are readily accessible, and ultimately, it is the child that suffers. A lack of suitable support, which is personalised and correctly delivered at the right time, can have huge academic, emotional and mental impacts on a child, and later, their life chances.

The aim of this book is to help parents to secure the provisions for their children that they are entitled to. It has been arranged in such a way that, to each question, there is an answer based upon my knowledge and experience, in addition to references to laws or statutory documents that are relevant. Use this book in a way that helps you and your child. Hopefully someone will listen to you now.

I hope that it proves useful.

Chris.

www.senachieve.co.uk

SEN Achieve YouTube

Chapter 1 - SEN Provision

Abbreviation used	Document or legislation
SCOP	SEND Code of Practice 2015
CFA	Children and Families Act 2014
UNCRPD	The United Nations Convention on the Rights of Persons with Disabilities
TS	The Teaching Standards 2011
EAGE	Ensuring a good education for children who cannot attend school because of health needs 2013
SCWMC	Supporting pupils at school with medical conditions 2015
SA	School attendance 2020
EA	The Equality Act 2010
EAAS	The Equality Act 2010 and Schools 2014

1. Does my child need to have a diagnosis to be considered as having SEN or to be on the SEN register?

The simple answer is no. Many parents have contacted me saying that they have been told by a SENCo or class teacher that a child has to have a diagnosis to be classed as having any kind of 'SEN', or at least on a waiting list for an assessment. Another parent stated that they had been informed that a child must be at least two years behind to be placed on a SEN register. One parent even told me that a SENCo had told them that this is the law across all parts of the country.

This is not true...the law does not state this anywhere.

In fact, pages 15 and 16 of the SCOP states:

"A child or young person has SEN if they have a learning difficulty or disability which calls for special educational provision to be made for him or her.

A child of compulsory school age or a young person has a learning difficulty or disability if he or she:

• has a significantly greater difficulty in learning than the majority of others of the same age, or

• has a disability which prevents or hinders him or her from making use of facilities of a kind generally provided for others of the same age in mainstream schools or mainstream post-16 institutions".

I hope this helps to clarify things!

2.Does my child have a right to SEN provision?

Disappointingly many parents have told me that they have been advised that there is nothing or very little that a school can do to help or support their child, despite them being behind their peers, and in some cases, having various diagnoses.

In some instances, a lack of time has been quoted as a reason for not providing support, or "we have 30 other children to worry about". Other parents have stated to me that they have been told "We only have to support academic needs".

Such responses are not OK, they conflict with the expected teaching standards in addition to a child's rights under various laws. Indeed, the law is clear that local authorities and schools have legal obligations in terms of providing for children with SEN.

Page 25 of the SCOP states:

"High quality teaching that is differentiated and personalised will meet the individual needs of the majority of children and young people. Some children and young people need educational provision that is additional to or different from this.

This is special educational provision under Section 21 of the Children and Families Act 2014. Schools and colleges must use their best endeavours to ensure that such provision is made for those who need it. Special educational provision is underpinned by high quality teaching and is compromised by anything less".

Page 92 of the SCOP states:

"All children and young people are entitled to an appropriate education, one that is appropriate to their needs, promotes high standards and the fulfilment of potential.

This should enable them to:

• achieve their best

• become confident individuals living fulfilling lives, and

• make a successful transition into adulthood, whether into employment, further or higher education or training.

Every school is required to identify and address the SEN of the pupils that they support.

Mainstream schools, which in this chapter includes maintained schools and academies that are not special schools, maintained nursery schools, 16 to19 academies, alternative provision academies and Pupil Referral Units (PRUs), must:

• use their best endeavours to make sure that a child with SEN gets the support they need – this means doing everything they can to meet children and young people's SEN

• ensure that children and young people with SEN engage in the activities of

the school alongside pupils who do not have SEN".

Section 66 (2) of the CFA states:

"If a registered pupil or a student at a school or other institution has special educational needs, the appropriate authority must, in exercising its functions in relation to the school or other institution, use its best endeavours to secure that the special educational provision called for by the pupil's or student's special educational needs is made".

Also, it is worth looking at the following:

- Article 3 of the UNCROC
- Articles 7 and 24 of the UNCRPD.

3.Do schools have to follow a process to identify SEN and SEN needs?

Yes, they do!

All children are entitled to an appropriate education that is suitable to their needs - for this to happen, a process of assessment, planning, provision and evaluation is required for children with SEN. This four-stage process helps to ensure that things are done in a comprehensive, consistent and personalised way that works for your child.

Before plans and actions are put in place for a child, assessments of need have to take place first. Further, once the subsequent plans have been made and executed, they need to be evaluated to make sure that they are right for that child; in other words, do the strategies actually work? A parent once told me that their child had been attending the same intervention group for over two years and had made very little progress, yet the school was still ploughing on with no or little changes. This has no value to the child, and uses financial and human resources that could be used in alternative ways to the benefit of the child's education and well-being.

Further, for provision to be suitable and effective, and ultimately in the best interests of the child, the identification and support of SEN at an early stage is also essential. Not only does this support the likelihood of needs being understood and provision being appropriate as soon as is possible, but it also reduces the emotional impact that an ineffective education can have on a child and their family.

When there are concerns around SEN, initial discussions should focus around what the key issues are, any diagnoses that have been made (if applicable) and associated reports, in addition to related rates of progress and levels of attainment. Ideally these discussions will involve the parent, class teacher and SENCo, and if appropriate, the child or young person themselves.

The action that is taken next, including any support that is introduced, will be in part influenced by any diagnoses and/ or assessments that are already in place. If it is considered that a child or young person does have SEN, schools should put in place what is called 'SEN Support'.

As described above, SEN Support is a 4-part cycle that should be personalised to the child, specific, up to date and reflective, changing with time in response to the child's needs, progress and the impact of any support.

Page 100 to 102 of the SCOP explains the 4 stages of the cycle.

Each one is described in brief here:

Assess – This stage involves the clear identification of a child's needs. It may involve regular assessments, specialised assessments, observations, conversations and referrals to, and reports from, external professionals.

Plan – Based on the assessments that have been performed and the needs that have been subsequently identified, the support for a child is then planned. The child or young person, parents, teacher(s) and SENCo should all be involved. The plan should be clearly communicated to the parent.

Do – This is the stage during which the plan is actioned. The class teacher retains responsibility for the pupil, in terms of planning, progress and attainment.

Review – As with the previous 3 stages, this stage is essential. There is no point in a child receiving support if it is of no benefit to them. The impact of any support should be reviewed in line with an agreed date. The analyses that is performed should be shared with parents and, with the views of the parent, should feed back into the assessment and planning stages.

Page 94 of the SCOP states:

"All schools should have a clear approach to identifying and responding to SEN".

4. I have paid for private assessments to be performed, but I have been told that they do not count! Is this true?

This is one of the questions that I get asked the most. Parents across the country have reported to me that they have been informed of this by local authority staff, head teachers, SENCos and class teachers. One parent stated that they had been told "our school does not accept private assessments"; another said that they have been told "our local authority used to accept them, but not anymore".

The bottom line is this: if an assessment has been carried out by someone who has the necessary qualifications, who has used the correct procedures and (where necessary) is a member of the appropriate organisations, then it counts.

Further, the law does not state who a professional who carries out an assessment has to work for! It is also worthy of note that I have never heard a judge at the SEND First Tier Tribunal question the use of private assessments on the basis that it was paid for by a parent.

It is very ironic that this query comes my way so much, as it is often alongside reports from parents that they have been asked to accept in-school assessments that have been performed by (in some cases) completely untrained staff. Plus, some schools contract work from independent assessors outside of the local authority themselves.

So, if you have paid for an assessment and are told that the assessment and/ or diagnosis does not count, my advice is this:

1. Ask the person who is refusing to accept the assessment and/ or diagnosis to write a position statement, outlining their decision and reasoning, to yourself and the professional(s) who conducted the assessments/ diagnosis.

2. Speak to the professional(s) who performed the assessment and/ or diagnosis, inform them of what you have been told, and provide them with a copy of the position statement.

3. Hopefully, the professional(s) will respond accordingly, in writing, endorsing the work that they have done.

Obviously always do your research on who you use to assess your child.

Page 102 of SCOP states:

"Where a pupil continues to make less than expected progress, despite evidence-based support and interventions that are matched to the pupil's area of need, the school should consider involving specialists, including those secured by the school itself or from outside agencies.

A school should always involve a specialist where a pupil continues to make little or no progress or where they continue to work at levels substantially below those expected of pupils of a similar age despite evidence-based SEN support delivered by appropriately trained staff".

Page 103 states:

"Where assessment indicates that support from specialist services is required, it is important that children and young people receive it as quickly as possible".

5.Does a school need to have a SENCo?

A SENCo is a critical point of contact for parents, ideally being there to listen, advise, signpost and help to develop a way forwards for your child.

However, all too often I am told that when parents have asked to speak to their child's SENCo, they are told that they are simply not available. Some have been told that the school doesn't have one at the moment, or even that they are just another teacher, so there is no value in talking to them!

I have also, worryingly, had an increasing number of calls from parents whose children attend high school, and who have never met the school SENCo, despite their children being in year ten or eleven!

These situations are unacceptable. Though they can share one, mainstream schools must have a SENCo, it is not an option. Further, the organisation of the school should be done in such a way that the SENCo has sufficient time to fulfil the position which they are employed to do.

Page 108 of the SCOP states:

"The SENCO must be a qualified teacher working at the school.

Governing bodies of maintained mainstream schools and the proprietors of mainstream academy schools (including free schools) must ensure that there is a qualified teacher designated as SENCO for the school".

Page 109 states:

"The school should ensure that the SENCO has sufficient time and resources to carry out these functions. This should include providing the SENCO with sufficient administrative support and time away from teaching to enable them to fulfil their responsibilities in a similar way to other important strategic roles within a school".

"It may be appropriate for a number of smaller primary schools to share a SENCO employed to work across the individual schools, where they meet the other requirements set out in this chapter of the Code. Schools can consider this arrangement where it secures sufficient time away from teaching and sufficient administrative support to enable the

SENCO to fulfil the role effectively for the total registered pupil population across all of the schools involved".

If you are unable to speak to the school SENCo for any reason, my advice is to put your request for a meeting in an email; this way, you have proof of exactly what you have asked for and when. If you do not get an appropriate response, I would email the head teacher next. If an appropriate response is still not forthcoming, I would then ask for the contact details of the Chair of Governors and the Governor who is allocated responsibility for SEN in the school. You could also contact the SEN department of your local education authority.

Section 67 (2) of the CFA states:

"The appropriate authority must designate a member of staff at the school (to be known as the "SEN co-ordinator") as having responsibility for co-ordinating the provision for pupils with special educational needs".

6.What does (or should) a SENCo do?

The SENCo fills (and should provide) an essential and valuable role in a school. Broadly speaking, this role is to ensure that all the children with any kind of SEN have the opportunity to access and enjoy the curriculum and everyday life in the school, and ultimately, to fulfil their potential.

More specifically, the role involves coordinating and monitoring the support available to children with SEN in the school, liaising closely with pupils and their parents, engaging with external professionals and often compiling and monitoring in school provision and progress data.

Page 108 of the SCOP states:

"The SENCO has day-to-day responsibility for the operation of SEN policy and coordination of specific provision made to support individual pupils with SEN, including those who have EHC plans".

"The SENCO provides professional guidance to colleagues and will work closely with staff, parents and other agencies. The SENCO should be aware of the provision in the Local Offer and be able to work with professionals providing a support role to families to ensure that pupils with SEN receive appropriate support and high-quality teaching".

7.The SENCo has said "This school year doesn't matter, things are all repeated next year". Is this true?

I have been told this a few times now by parents across the country. This is unbelievable and wholly unacceptable.

EVERY child is entitled by law to an appropriate education. It is also of critical importance that needs are identified and met early. It is by no means OK for any child to be expected to sit in a class whilst their education passes them by. Not only would this not provide them with an education, but the impact on a child's emotional and mental health could be huge and long lasting. These quotes from the SEND Code of Practice maybe of use to you here:

Page 94 of the SCOP states:

"Benefits of early identification are widely recognised – identifying need at the earliest point and then making effective provision improves long-term outcomes for the child or young person".

Page 92 of the SCOP sates:

"All children and young people are entitled to an appropriate education, one that is appropriate to their needs, promotes high standards and the fulfilment of potential".

8. Is it reasonable for lessons to be adjusted to the needs of a child?

Yes, it is! Many parents that I have spoken to over the months have said that they have been told that their child's teacher does not have the time to adjust lesson content to meet the needs of their child, or that they do not have the strategies nor the knowledge that are needed to teach their child. These situations are not acceptable at all. Indeed, many statutory documents make clear reference to the obligations that a school has.

Page 99 of the SCOP states:

"Teachers are responsible and accountable for the progress and development of the pupils in their class, including where pupils access support from teaching assistants or specialist staff".

"High quality teaching, differentiated for individual pupils, is the first step in responding to pupils who have or may have SEN".

Pages 11 and 12 of the TS states:

A teacher must:

"Adapt teaching to respond to the strengths and needs of all pupils

- know when and how to differentiate appropriately, using approaches which enable pupils to be taught effectively

- have a secure understanding of how a range of factors can inhibit pupils' ability to learn, and how best to overcome these

- demonstrate an awareness of the physical, social and intellectual development of children, and know how to adapt teaching to support pupils' education at different stages of development

- have a clear understanding of the needs of all pupils, including those with special educational needs; those of high ability; those with English as an additional language; those with disabilities; and be able to use and evaluate distinctive teaching approaches to engage and support them".

9.What if the school refuses to put things in place for my child?

Unfortunately, this is a question I get asked almost on a weekly basis. If you believe that your child has SEN and requires support, this is what I would do:

1. **Ask for the reasons** - As a parent, the first thing that I would do is ask for the reasons for the decision to not put additional support in place in writing. Make the request in writing/ by email, and address it for the attention of the school SENCo. You could request a reply within 5 school days. This then gives you proof of exactly what has been said should you have to take things further.

2. **Request a meeting** – In the same email, I would request a meeting with the school SENCo, and possibly the class teacher, to discuss your concerns further.

3. **Prepare for the meeting** – Always prepare for a school meeting, this way you are less likely to forget the things that you want to say! Make a list of any diagnoses your child

has, their areas of difficulty, your key concerns, and the support that you wish to be put in place and why.

4. **The meeting** – Use this time to go through each of the points on your list. Stay calm and get your points across. Do not feel rushed, this is your chance to be the voice of your child.

   If support cannot be offered, ask why. For any support that is offered, always ask who will be delivering it, how often and how the impact will be monitored and by whom. Also, ask how this will be documented, shared with you and reviewed.

   Finally, set a date for a review meeting, perhaps in 4 to 6 weeks. Make notes of what has been said. If the school takes minutes, ask for a copy or an overview of them before you leave.

5. **The next step** – If a school still refuses to put provision in place for your child's SEN, your next option is to inform the head teacher and ask them to ensure that appropriate

provision is put in place for your child. If you consider it necessary, you could use the formal complaints procedure of the school. There are a lot of directives in place to protect your child, some of which are quoted in this chapter, especially under question 2 (above).

6. **Going further** – Hopefully, doing the above will secure the provision that your child needs and is entitled to. If not, you have other options available. These could include contacting and informing:

a. The local authority
b. Your local MP
c. Using the local authority complaint procedure
d. Ofsted
e. The Department for Education

And/ or:

f. You may have a case to lodge an appeal with the SEND First Tier Tribunal on the basis of discrimination by schools or local authorities in relation to a child's disability.

10.What is the local offer?

Many parents contact me confused about something called the 'local offer'.

The SEND Code of Practice states that all local authorities must develop and publish a local offer, this is not an option. Indeed, the contents of what must be included are set out in Schedule 2 of the SEND Regulations 2014. The offer consists of information about all the services that are available to support children with SEN and/ or a disability within the area of the local authority.

What many families are unaware of, is that the local authority has a duty to involve children with SEN or disabilities and their parents in planning the contents of the offer, how best to publish it and reviewing it. I hope that this is happening!

Page 59 of the SCOP states:

"Local authorities **must** publish a Local Offer, setting out in one place information about provision they expect to be available across education, health and social care for children and young people in their area who have SEN or are disabled, including those who do not have

Education, Health and Care (EHC) plans. In setting out what they 'expect to be available', local authorities should include provision which they believe will actually be available".

It is also worth viewing Section 30 of the CFA!

11.Is my child entitled to an education if they are off sick?

Yes, they are!

Many parents have contacted me asking what the position is when their child is signed off sick by a GP, but no educational provision is being made for them. In some cases, this has been despite repeated requests for provision being made.

Parents have also told me of schools and local authorities who pass the buck onto the other. Make sure that you put your requests in emails – this way you can prove what you have said and when.

Page 7 of EAGE states:

"Children unable to attend school because of health needs should be able to access suitable and flexible education appropriate to their needs. The nature of the provision must be responsive to the demands of what may be a changing health status".

Page 6 of EAGE states that:

"LAs are responsible for arranging suitable full-time education for children of compulsory school age who, because of illness, would not receive suitable education without such provision. This applies whether or not the child is on the role of a school and whatever the type of school they attend. It applies to children who are pupils in Academies, Free Schools, special schools and independent schools as well as those in maintained schools".

"Where full-time education would not be in the best interests of a particular child because of reasons relating to their physical or mental health, LAs should provide part-time education on a basis they consider to be in the child's best interests. Full and part-time education should still aim to achieve good academic attainment particularly in English, Maths and Science".

Interestingly, on page 5 it also states that local authorities should not:

"Withhold or reduce the provision, or type of provision, for a child because of how much it will cost (meeting the child's needs and providing a good education must be the determining factors)".

"Have lists of health conditions which dictate whether or not they will arrange education for children or inflexible policies which result in children going without suitable full-time education (or as much education as their health condition allows them to participate in)".

12.My child has SEN, should she have an IEP?

Children with SEN should have provisions put in place for them. However, how these provisions are presented to parents is not set in law. Local authorities and schools therefore have flexibility in terms of how they present this information, and what they call these documents. Some names that are used include:

- IEPs – Individual Education Plans
- PSPs – Personal Support Plans
- One Page Profiles
- One Plans
- Pupil Passports.

I have also known of some schools that do not use any document at all, and parents have reported to me that they have been told that they do not need to have one. So where do you stand?

Well, this is what the SEND Code of Practice says:

Page 101 of SCOP states:

- "Where it is decided to provide a pupil with SEN support, the parents must be formally notified, although parents should have already been involved in forming the assessment of needs as outlined above.

- The teacher and the SENCO should agree in consultation with the parent and the pupil the adjustments, interventions and support to be put in place, as well as the expected impact on progress, development or behaviour, along with a clear date for review".

- "Parents should be fully aware of the planned support and interventions and, where appropriate, plans should seek parental involvement to reinforce or contribute to progress at home".

Section 68 (2) of the CFA states:

"The appropriate authority for the school must inform the child's parent or the young person that special educational provision is being made for the child or young person".

So, if a school was to do the above, it would follow that this would be documented somewhere, and, that this should be shared with the parents!

As a parent, therefore, you are fully within your rights to ask for the details of all support that is being put in place for your child, the dates for review, and how you as a parent can support the plan in the home.

13.My child has medical needs, he needs a healthcare plan, does the school have to put one in place to support him?

This is a topic that surprises me a lot, in that parents have reported to me some very poor responses that they have received from staff. Some have told me that they were advised that "school's do not have to use them anymore", and "we only use them as a favour to parents". Such comments are shocking and conflict with the law completely.

Schools have a legal duty, as set out in the Children and Families Act of 2014. There should also be a clear process in place for supporting children with such needs, in terms of what the school must do once they have been notified of health needs, the roles and responsibilities of the school staff, in addition to how staff will be supported and trained.

Here are some very useful quotes that may help you if you find yourself in this position.

Section 100 (1) of the CFA states:

"The appropriate authority for a school to which this section applies must make arrangements for supporting pupils at the school with medical conditions".

Page 4 of SCWMC states:

"Pupils at school with medical conditions should be properly supported so that they have full access to education, including school trips and physical education".

Page 7 states:

"The governing body must ensure that arrangements are in place to support pupils with medical conditions. In doing so it should ensure that such children can access and enjoy the same opportunities at school as any other child".

Page 12 states:

"The governing body should ensure that the school's policy clearly identifies the roles and responsibilities of all those involved in the arrangements they make to support pupils at school with medical conditions".

Page 17 states:

"The school's policy should be clear that any member of school staff providing support to a pupil with medical needs should have received suitable training".

Page 94 of the SCOP states:

"The Children and Families Act 2014 places a duty on maintained schools and academies to make arrangements to support pupils with medical conditions. Individual healthcare plans will normally specify the type and level of support required to meet the medical needs of such pupils. Where children and young people also have SEN, their provision should be planned and delivered in a co-ordinated way with the healthcare plan. Schools are required to have regard to statutory guidance 'Supporting pupils at school with medical conditions'".

14.Can my child be placed on a reduced timetable for several months?

This is another question that I get asked frequently. I've been told of some children being placed on a part-time timetable for several months, and in some cases, over a year.

In some ways, and for some children and young people, part-time timetables can be useful. They can give a child the chance to engage with school for a smaller amount of time that allows them to be successful. This can, in some cases, build confidence, help to ease anxiety and build a more positive outlook towards attending school.

However, part time timetables should be progressive, agreed by the parent and the school, and for a reasonable period of time. The Department for Education are very clear that there must be a time limit and a reduced timetable must not be seen as a long-term solution.

In response, to the question "can a child be placed on a reduced timetable?", the Department for Education document 'School Attendance' (2020) states:

- "As a rule, no. All pupils of compulsory school age are entitled to a full-time education. In very exceptional circumstances there may be a need for a temporary part-time timetable to meet a pupil's individual needs.

- For example, where a medical condition prevents a pupil from attending full-time education and a part-time timetable is considered as part of a re-integration package.

- A part-time timetable must not be treated as a long-term solution.

- Any pastoral support programme or other agreement must have a time limit by which point the pupil is expected to attend full-time or be provided with alternative provision".

15.Can I inform Ofsted about my views relating to the provision my child receives in school?

Yes, you can, and you can do so at any time, you do not need to wait until a school is being inspected!

Take a look at the Ofsted website for more information.

16. Is my child protected under the Equality Act of 2010?

Many parents have contacted me stating that, despite their child having a diagnosis, their school have told them that they cannot provide for them, in terms of lesson planning, general SEN provision and even in terms of going on school trips. The answers to questions 2, 8 and 9 in this chapter are relevant here. In addition, it is also likely that your child has protection under the Equality Act of 2010.

To simplify the answer to this question, I have broken it down into four separate sections.

a. So, first of all, in terms of the law, what is the definition of a disability?

Section 6 of the EA states:

"A person (P) has a disability if—

(a)P has a physical or mental impairment, and

(b)the impairment has a substantial and long-term adverse effect on P's ability to carry out normal day-to-day activities".

Therefore, under this definition, ASD, SPD, ADHD, dyslexia and dyscalculia would all be covered.

b. Next, if a child is protected by the act, what does this mean for them?

The Act says that it is unlawful for a school to discriminate against or victimise a pupil:

- in the way in which it provides education for the pupil;
- in the way in which it provides the pupil access to a benefit, facility or service;
- by not providing education for a pupil;
- by not providing the pupil access to a benefit, facility or service; or
- by subjecting the pupil to any other detriment.

A school's obligation to pupils covers everything that a school provides for pupils including things such as extracurricular and leisure activities, afterschool and homework clubs, sports activities and trips off site.

c. OK, so what about reasonable adjustments?

The law places a duty on schools to make reasonable adjustments for children with a disability. A reasonable adjustment is basically an adjustment or step that help a child avoid a disadvantage that someone with a disability could otherwise face in a given situation.

Page 26 of the EAAS states:

"The duty to make reasonable adjustments applies only to disabled people. For schools the duty is summarised as follows:

• Where something a school does places a disabled pupil at a disadvantage compared to other pupils then the school must take reasonable steps to try and avoid that disadvantage.

• Schools will be expected to provide an auxiliary aid or service for a disabled pupil when it would be reasonable to do so and if such an aid would alleviate any substantial disadvantage that the pupil faces in comparison to non-disabled pupils".

Page 93 of the SCOP states:

"All schools have duties under the Equality Act 2010 towards individual disabled children and young people. They **must** make reasonable adjustments, including the provision of auxiliary aids and services for disabled children, to prevent them being put at a substantial disadvantage".

d. Finally, you may have heard about 'positive actions'...what are these?

Some parents have said to me that school staff have told them that it would be "unfair" to make an adjustment to an event or process for a child with a disability. When I have spoken to such staff, it has become apparent that they have not heard of positive actions. Positive actions basically make it lawful to treat a child with a disability more favourably, to help put them on a more level playing field as children who do not have a disability.

Page 11 of the EAAS states:

"The law on disability discrimination is different from the rest of the Act in a number of ways. In particular, it works in only one direction – that is to say, it protects disabled people but not people who are not disabled. This means that schools are allowed to treat disabled pupils more favourably than non-disabled pupils, and in some cases are required to do so, by making reasonable adjustments to put them on a more level footing with pupils without disabilities".

Page 24 states:

"However, the provisions relating to disability discrimination are different in that you may, and often must, treat a disabled person more favourably than a person who is not disabled and may have to make changes to your practices to ensure, as far as is reasonably possible, that a disabled person can benefit from what you offer to the same extent that a person without that disability can".

Chapter 2 – EHCPs

Abbreviation used	Document or legislation
CFA	Children and Families Act 2014
SCOP	SEND Code of Practice 2015
SENDR	The SEND Regulations 2014
TEA	The Education Act 1996

1.What is an EHCP?

EHCP stands for 'Education, Health & Care Plan'.

- EHCPs were introduced in 2014.

- The EHCP is a document which lists all of the assessed education, health and social care needs of a child, in addition to the support that is needed to support those needs.

- EHCPs document the views, interests and aspirations of the parents and child/ young person.

- They are designed to secure the best possible outcomes for a child and to help them prepare for adulthood.

- An EHCP is legally binding, in that any provision which is stated that a child needs must be funded and provided.

- The purpose of the EHCP is to secure the correct support for a child, in order to help achieve the best outcomes for them, across, where applicable, education, health and social care.

- The contents of an EHCP are reviewed every year.

- Any professional who reads an EHCP should be able to gain a full understanding of the child's needs and what provision is required to support them.

2.EHCPs...Are they worth it?

A lot of parents have phoned me asking if it is worth trying to secure an EHCP for their child, especially as they say they have been told that it can be a long and difficult process.

Some parents have also said that they have told that an EHCP is "just a piece of paper2, that an EHCP "is for children with more needs than yours" or that "we do not issue them at the moment". None of these statements are relevant. If they were made in relation to my child, I would not attach any significance to them whatsoever. This is because EHCPs are statutory documents, the way that they are managed and their contents are embedded in law. Neither a local authority or a school have the right to ignore these laws.

So, are EHCPs worth it? If a child or young person has complex SEN then, in my opinion, yes, they are worth it.

This opinion is based upon the following reasons:

a. The educational provisions stipulated within an EHCP have to be provided by law (as per Section 42 of the Children and Families Act, 2014).

b. The Children and Families Act allows parents the right to request a particular school or college for their child or young person – this could be a mainstream or a specialist school.

c. EHCPs help to coordinate the range of services, professionals and support in place for a child.

d. An EHCP can, if appropriate, support a child into adulthood.

If you genuinely believe that your child needs an EHCP, go through the process of application and stand up for what you believe is right for your child.

3. I've been told that children have to be 2 years behind to get an EHCP! Is this true?

I hear this a lot, and the simple answer is no!

One parent even told me that a school had said that only children who are 4 years behind will qualify for an EHCP. This is nonsense. Nowhere in the law does it state that a child must be a specific amount of time behind in order to meet the criteria for an EHCP. Further, local authorities must not apply blanket policies that apply to every child – every child is different!

In fact, the criteria for conducting an EHCP assessment (the first stage in the EHCP process) is that the local authority believes, after looking at the evidence, a child has or may have SEN, and that it may be necessary for SEN provision to made in accordance to an EHCP.

Section 36 (8) of the CFA states:

"The local authority must secure an EHC needs assessment for the child or young person if, after having regard to any views expressed and evidence submitted under subsection (7), the authority is of the opinion that—

(a)the child or young person has or may have special educational needs, and

(b)it may be necessary for special educational provision to be made for the child or young person in accordance with an EHC plan".

Page 146 of the SCOP states:

"Local authorities must not apply a 'blanket' policy to particular groups of children or certain types of need, as this would prevent the consideration of a child's or young person's needs individually and on their merits".

4. What age does an EHCP cover?

The age covered by an EHCP, if considered necessary, is 0 to 25.

5. I'm a parent, can I apply for an EHCP for my child?

A question that I often get asked by parents is whether or not they, as parents, are able to make a request for an EHC Needs Assessment themselves. I've been informed by many parents that they have been told that only a school can apply! This is simply not true.

As a parent you have a right to apply for an EHC Needs Assessment yourself, this is actually called a 'specific right'. It is highly advisable to discuss with the school that you are planning to do this, as it keeps things open and maintains a flow of communication between you and school.

In my opinion the key benefit of submitting the application yourself, is that the moment you submit the application, the start of the 20-week time limit is triggered. This avoids the delay that may be caused by waiting for the school to submit an application.

Pages 143 and 144 of the SCOP state:

"The following people have a specific right to ask a local authority to conduct an education, health and care needs assessment for a child or young person aged between 0 and 25:

• the child's parent

• a young person over the age of 16 but under the age of 25, and

• a person acting on behalf of a school or post-16 institution (this should ideally be with the knowledge and agreement of the parent or young person where possible)".

"In addition, anyone else can bring a child or young person who has (or may have) SEN to the attention of the local authority, particularly where they think an EHC needs assessment may be necessary. This could include, for example, foster carers, health and social care professionals, early years practitioners, youth offending teams or probation services, those responsible for education in custody, school or college staff or a family friend. Bringing a child or young person to the attention of the local authority will be undertaken on an individual basis where there are specific concerns. This should be done with the knowledge and, where possible, agreement of the child's parent or the young person".

"Children and young people under 19 in youth custodial establishments also have the right to request an assessment for an EHC plan. The child's parent, the young person themselves or the professionals working with them can ask the home local authority to conduct an EHC needs assessment while they are still detained".

Section 36 of the CFA states:

"A request for a local authority in England to secure an EHC needs assessment for a child or young person may be made to the authority by the child's parent, the young person or a person acting on behalf of a school or post-16 institution".

6.If I apply for an EHCP assessment myself, what should I include?

If you decide to apply for an EHCP assessment for your child, here are some practical steps that you could follow:

a. Look online for the form or template used by your local education authority. If you search for 'EHCP assessment request' and type the name of the authority, it should come up!

b. Contact your child's school and ask for all of the academic data that they have for your child, including their attainment (where they are at) and progress data (the rate or measure by which they have moved on), for the present and historically.

c. In addition, ask for any information they have regarding broader aspects of your child's presentation and progress, including their communication and interaction, social skills, behaviour, physical and sensory needs, emotional and mental health.

d. Ask the school for a list of the support that has been put in place for your child (current and historical), and if possible, the costs of any such support and the impacts.

e. When you complete your form or letter, include as much detail as possible.

f. List any diagnoses that your child has, and how they affect your child.

g. Think about your child's areas of need, and try to present them under the four categories listed below (if they are applicable):

- **Communication and interaction** – this covers any issues relating to speech and language needs, and includes difficulties relating to ASD.
- **Cognition and learning** – this refers to difficulties which affect the rate at which a child learns, and can include issues relating to memory, processing speed, dyslexia and dyscalculia.

- **Sensory or physical needs** – this covers vision and hearing impairments, physical disabilities and sensory processing difficulties.
- **Social, emotional and mental health** – this covers issues relating to social skills, friendships and behaviour, in addition to anxiety and depression.

h. Make reference to (and include) any professional reports that you have. This could include medical reports, assessment or diagnostic reports, letters from a GP, CAMHS or the school.

i. When you email your documents to the local authority, ask for:
- Confirmation of receipt of your email

And,

- The name of the person (with contact details) who will be dealing with your application for assessment.

7.What happens once an application for an EHCP has been made?

    a. The moment an application has been submitted (I advise this is done by email) the **20-week** statutory process is started.

    b. The **local authority must then decide whether or not, in their view, an EHC Needs Assessment is necessary**; this decision must be made and parents informed **within 6 weeks** of the application.

    c. During this decision-making process, the local authority **must** have regard for the **views of the child and their parents, or the young person**.

    d. **If the local authority decide to assess** – a parent will be informed within 6 weeks of the application. A parent must then be given the opportunity to share their views and any relevant information during the assessment process.

e. **If the local authority decides not to assess** – a parent will be informed within 6 weeks of the application. A parent must also be informed of their right to appeal.

f. **EHCP assessment completed – decision to issue** – a draft plan will be put together and sent to parents. Parents at this point are given 15 days within which to share their views and school placement choice with the local authority.

g. **EHCP assessment completed – decision not to issue** - parents must be notified withing 16 weeks of the original application. A parent must again be informed of their right to appeal.

h. **Final Plan** – the EHCP must be issued to parents no later than 20 weeks from the date the application was submitted to the local authority.

8.How long does the whole EHCP process take?

A question that I often get asked is how long the whole EHCP process should take, once a request for assessment has been submitted. Some parents have told me that a local authority or school representative have said that the time limit for their area is 30 to 40 weeks. I have known EHCPs to take even longer, and in some cases up to two years. This is not acceptable; as stated above, clear timescales are set by the law. Schools and local authorities are not allowed to simply set their own timescales that exceed those that are embedded in the law. Therefore, there is a clear answer to this question - 20 weeks.

Page 157 of the SCOP states:

"The local authority should ensure it allows enough time to prepare the draft plan and complete the remaining steps in the process within the 20-week overall time limit within which it must issue the finalised EHC plan".

Page 152 of the SCOP states:

The exceptions to this include where:

• "appointments with people from whom the local authority has requested information are missed by the child or young person (this only applies to the duty on partners to comply with a request under the EHC needs assessment process within six weeks)

• the child/ young person is absent from the area for at least 4 weeks

• exceptional personal circumstances affect the child or his/her parent, or the young person, and

• the educational institution is closed for at least 4 weeks, which may delay the submission of information from the school or other institution (this does not apply to the duty on partners to comply with a request under the EHC needs assessment process within six weeks)".

Part 13 of the SENDR states:

"A local authority must send the finalised EHC plan to—

(a)the child's parent or to the young person;

(b)the governing body, proprietor or principal of any school, other institution or provider of relevant early years education named in the EHC plan; and

(c)to the responsible commissioning body,

as soon as practicable, and in any event within 20 weeks of the local authority receiving a request for an EHC needs assessment".

9.My child's EHCP is taking too long! What can I do?

If a local authority is going beyond the timescales that are set in law, there are a few options available to you.

At first it is advisable to contact your EHCP representative at the local authority. If this does not bring a solution to the problem, you could contact their manager next, and/ or the head of education at your local authority.

If this also proves unsuccessful, you could use the complaint procedure of your local authority, and if you feel that the delay is affecting your child's access to an education, you may have a case to lodge an appeal with the SEND First Tier Tribunal on the basis of discrimination related to a child's disability.

10. What sections must be in an EHCP?

EHCPs have to contain certain sections by law. A local authority cannot choose which ones to include and which to leave out. However, the local authority can choose how it considers the best way to present them, in other words, there is not a set template that must be used.

Opposite is a guide to the sections and what they contain.

Section	Contents
A	The views, interests and aspirations of the child, their parents or the young person.
B	The special educational needs (SEN) of the child or young person.
C	The health care needs that are related to the SEN.
D	The social care needs that relate to the SEN and/ or disability.
E	The outcomes or targets for the child or young person, both short and long term.
F	The SEN provision required by the child or young person.
G	The health provision reasonably required by the learning difficulties or disabilities which result in the child or young person having SEN. If an Individual Health Care Plan has been made for the child or young person, this should also be included.
H1	Social care which must be made for a child or young person under 18 resulting from section 2 of the Chronically Sick and Disabled Persons Act 1970.
H2	Other social care provision reasonably required by the learning difficulties or disabilities which result in the child or young person having SEN. This will include any adult social care provision being provided to meet a young person's eligible needs (through a statutory care and support plan) under the Care Act 2014.
I	The name and type of the educational establishment to be attended by the child or young person.

J	The Personal Budget used to secure the provision identified.
K	The information gathered during the EHC needs assessment must be attached (in appendices).

11.What is the draft plan?

- Before the final EHCP is issued for a child, a draft plan is issued first. This is an important opportunity for you to share your opinion on the contents! It is the parents' chance to share their views and requests before the final plan is issued and distributed.

- The draft plan contains all of the information, needs, outcomes and provisions that the local authority intend to put into the final plan, with the exception of the school to be attended.

- The draft plan gives parents the chance to consider the contents of the plan, suggest any changes, and to request the school that they would like their child to attend.

- Parents must be given at least 15 days to give their views about a draft plan.

- Local authority staff must also be available during these 15 days to meet with parents or a young person if they wish to.

- My advice here is to use this opportunity to speak up and say if there is anything that you are not happy about. Also, as always, ensure that you put your views in an email, then you can prove exactly what you have said and when.

Page 171 of the SCOP states:

"The local authority **must** send the draft EHC plan (including the appendices containing the advice and information gathered during the EHC needs assessment) to the child's parent or to the young person and give them at least 15 days to give views and make representations on the content. During this period, the local authority must make its officers available for a meeting with the child's parent or the young person on request if they wish to discuss the content of the draft EHC plan".

Part 13 of the SENDR states:

"When a local authority sends a draft plan to a child's parent or young person it must—

(a)give them at least 15 days, beginning with the day on which the draft plan was served, in which to—

(i)make representations about the content of the draft plan, and to request that a particular school or other institution be named in the plan; and

(ii)require the local authority to arrange a meeting between them and an officer of the local authority at which the draft plan can be discussed; and

(b)advise them where they can find information about the schools and colleges that are available for the child or young person to attend".

12. What is a personal budget?

Personal budgets seem to cause a lot of confusion, amongst many of the parents and professionals that I have worked with. I have also found, unfortunately, that the information given about personal budgets, and what has been reportedly been given, is often vague and in some cases inaccurate.

Hopefully this will help to clear things up a little:

- A **personal budget is the amount of money** that a local authority believes is needed to secure the provision identified within an EHCP for a child.

- If a parent asks for a personal budget to be prepared, the law states that a local authority must do this (see below).

- The money identified within a personal budget can then be used in one of four different ways; these include:

a. **Direct payments** – this is where money is paid directly to the parent for them to use to commission services or equipment to support their child in line with the EHCP.

b. **An arrangement** – this is where the local authority, school or college holds the money and uses it accordingly to meet the needs of the child in line with the EHCP.

c. **Third party arrangements** – in this case the money is transferred to and manged by a person or organisation on behalf of the child's parents or the young person.

d. **A combination of the above.**

Part 49 of the CFA states:

"A local authority that maintains an EHC plan, or is securing the preparation of an EHC plan, for a child or young person must prepare a personal budget for him or her if asked to do so by the child's parent or the young person".

13.How do I apply for a personal budget?

- The usual time to request the details of a personal budget and to make requests regarding how it is managed is during the draft phase, or at an EHCP review – as a parent you have a right to make this request.

- A request for a direct payment does not have to be granted by a local authority, if it considers that the separation of funds is not suitable, and/ or this would be an inefficient use of the authority's resources.

14. Reviewing an EHC plan - Does my local authority have to review my child's EHCP every year?

I've taken quite a few calls from parents who are concerned that the date for an annual review has passed by several months, sometimes by 6 or more, and that they are having difficulty securing a review with the professionals involved with their child. This is not acceptable, as an EHCP has to be reviewed at least every 12 months. This is not an option; it has to be done. For children under 5, the plan must be reviewed at least every 3 to 6 months!

Page 198 of the SCOP states:

"Local authorities should consider reviewing an EHC plan for a child under five at least every three to six months to ensure that the provision continues to be appropriate".

Page 194 states:

"EHC plans should be used to actively monitor children and young people's progress towards their outcomes and longer-term aspirations. They **must** be reviewed by the local authority as a minimum every 12 months".

Page 194 also states:

"Reviews must focus on the child or young person's progress towards achieving the outcomes specified in the EHC plan.

The review must also consider whether these outcomes and supporting targets remain appropriate".

Page 195 states:

"The local authority should provide a list of children and young people who will require a review of their EHC plan that term to all headteachers and principals of schools, colleges and other institutions attended by children or young people with EHC plans, at least two weeks before the start of each term".

Section 44 of the CFA states:

"A local authority must review an EHC plan that it maintains—

(a)in the period of 12 months starting with the date on which the plan was first made, and (b)in each subsequent period of 12 months starting with the date on which the plan was last reviewed under this section".

15. I would like to look at a specialist school for my daughter; when should I look?

There is not a definite time or point at which you should start looking at specialist schools for your child. My advice however is to start looking once the assessment process has begun, and then inform the local authority (by email) as soon as you are aware of your choice, along with your reasons. This gives them plenty of time to act. The formal point at which to notify the local authority is, however, at the draft EHCP stage.

There are lots of things you could do to help make your decision; these include:

- Looking at the school website
- Looking at information about the school on the Ofsted website
- Reading the school's SEND Information report and/or SEND Policy on the school website
- Going a on a tour or a virtual tour of the school (if possible)
- Speaking to the head teacher
- Speaking to other parents who have experience of the school.

16.I requested a place in a special school for my son. The school that I asked for was not named in the EHCP; when I asked why, I was told that there are not enough spaces! Is this OK?

This is one of the most common questions that I get asked. So many parents tell me that they have been told that their child's needs cannot be met in their mainstream school due to their needs - some even have this is writing. However, they also tell me that they have been informed by the local authority that their child cannot get the provision they need because there are not enough spaces, so the child has to stay where they are. This is not good enough.

All children are entitled to an appropriate education, simply saying that there are not enough spaces is not a valid justification for not providing a child with an education to which they are legally entitled. Section 9 of the TEA 1996 actually states how a child should be educated in line with a parents' wishes. Indeed, I have helped many parents to secure the school placement that they want for their child.

If a parent has requested a place at a specialist school for their child, a tribunal (if things went that far) would have to be convinced that:

A. The education provided would be suitable to the child.
B. The education of the child at that school would not adversely impact the education of others or the efficient use of resources.

This is what the statutory documents say...

Page 92 of the SCOP states:

"All children and young people are entitled to an appropriate education, one that is appropriate to their needs, promotes high standards and the fulfilment of potential".

Section 9 of the TEA states:

"In exercising or performing all their respective powers and duties under the Education Acts, the Secretary of State and local authorities shall have regard to the general principle that pupils are to be educated in accordance with the wishes of their parents, so far as that is compatible with the provision of efficient instruction and training and the avoidance of unreasonable public expenditure".

Section 39 of the CFA states:

"The local authority must secure that the EHC plan names the school or other institution specified in the request, unless subsection (4) applies.

(4)This subsection applies where—

(a)the school or other institution requested is unsuitable for the age, ability, aptitude or special educational needs of the child or young person concerned, or

(b)the attendance of the child or young person at the requested school or other institution would be incompatible with—

(i)the provision of efficient education for others, or

(ii)the efficient use of resources".

17. What happens if my child has an EHCP and I home educate my child?

Some parents choose to home educate their child. This is allowable under the Section 7 of the Education Act 1996. However, if a parent chooses to do this, the local authority is no longer responsible for securing the SEN provision identified in an EHCP. But the local authority is still responsible for maintaining the EHCP and they must be satisfied that the education needs of the child are being met by the alternative arrangements that are being made.

Section 7 of the TEA states:

"The parent of every child of compulsory school age shall cause him to receive efficient full-time education suitable—

(a) to his age, ability and aptitude, and

(b) to any special educational needs he may have, either by regular attendance at school or otherwise".

Chapter 3 – The Appeal and Tribunal Process

Ideally decisions relating to your child will be discussed and agreed upon informally.

However, there are times when it is necessary to take matters to the Tribunal service for a judge to make a decision as to what should happen going forwards.

This chapter covers the most common questions and issues that are raised when I speak to parents across the country.

Abbreviation used	Document or legislation
CFA	Children and Families Act 2014
SCOP	SEND Code of Practice 2015
SENDR	The SEND Regulations 2014
TEA	The Education Act 1996

1.What is disagreement resolution?

Disagreement resolution arrangements are made available by local authorities to parents as a relatively informal way of resolving disagreements, hopefully avoiding the need to take appeals further, and ultimately to the SEND Tribunal service.

Page 248 of the SCOP states:

"Local authorities must make disagreement resolution services available to parents and young people. Use of the disagreement resolution services is voluntary and has to be with the agreement of all parties. The service, while commissioned by it, must be independent of the local authority – no-one who is directly employed by a local authority can provide disagreement resolution services".

It is important to note here that, if you feel that you do not wish to use this process, page 250 of the SCOP states:

"A decision by parents and young people not to use disagreement resolution services has no effect on their right to appeal to the Tribunal and no inference will be drawn by the Tribunal if the parties to a disagreement have not used the disagreement resolution services.

Section 57 of the CFA 2014 underpins this aspect of a local authority's duties.

2. What is mediation?

The SCOP emphasises that disagreement resolution arrangements are designed to overcome disagreements about the performance of certain duties being performed, SEN provision, disagreements over health and social care provision and disagreements between health commissioners, and local authorities and are voluntary for both parties.

The process of mediation is, however, performed in relation to decisions about EHC needs assessments and EHCPs.

Page 252 of the SCOP states:

"Local authorities must make arrangements for parents and young people to receive information about mediation so that they can take part in mediation if they so choose before a possible appeal to the Tribunal".

Mediation is a less formal way of resolving differences in opinions relating to decisions that your child's local authority has made, before taking the matter to the tribunal service.

It would typically involve a mediator (who is independent), yourself (with support if you need it) and the local authority representative(s).

Sometimes matters can be resolved at this stage. After mediation, you are issued with a mediation certificate. If you are not satisfied with the outcome, you can then take the matter forward to the SEND Tribunal; you will need your mediation certificate to do this!

You have the option not to attend mediation but you must still contact the mediation service to obtain your mediation certificate (unless you are only appealing Section I (placement) within an EHCP). You will then receive your certificate within three working days.

3.What is the SEND tribunal?

The First Tier SEND Tribunal (or SEND Tribunal) is an independent national court service that hears appeals against local education authorities.

Page 259 of the SCOP states:

"The Tribunal hears appeals against decisions made by the local authorities in England in relation to children's and young people's EHC needs assessments and EHC plans. It also hears disability discrimination claims against schools and against local authorities when the local authority is the responsible body for a school".

4.When can I appeal?

Parents have two months within which they can appeal to the tribunal service, from the date of the letter on which the local authority gives their decision, or within one month of the date by which you have received your mediation certificate – whichever is later.

Page 253 of the SCOP states:

"The certificate will enable the parent or young person to lodge their appeal, either within two months of the original decision being sent by the local authority or within one month of receiving the certificate whichever is the later".

The SEND Tribunal must receive your appeal so that it is received within this timeframe. If for some reason you decide to appeal after this time, you can apply to the tribunal and apply under exceptional circumstances. Indeed, page 258 of the SCOP states:

"Where it is fair and just to do so the Tribunal has the power to use its discretion to accept appeals outside the two-month time limit".

5.Do the local authority have to tell me about my right to appeal?

Yes, they do, this is in line with their duties under the SEND Regulations 2014.

Indeed, following a decision not to conduct an EHCP assessment, issue or maintain an EHCP, or name a particular school, a local authority must inform the child's parent or young person of (though not exclusively):

- **their right to appeal that decision**
- **the time limits involved**
- **information regarding mediation.**

You rights to appeal are stated within Section 51 of the CFA 2014.

.

6.What can I appeal to the SEND Tribunal about?

You can appeal in the following situations:

- A local authority refuses to arrange an EHC assessment of a child or young person's special educational needs.

- A local authority refuses to issue an EHCP for a child or young person after completing an EHC assessment.

- You do not agree with the description of a child or young person's SEN (Section B) within an EHCP.

- You do not agree with the educational provision specified within an EHCP (Section F).

- You do not agree with the school or other institution named in the plan (Section I).

- The type of school or other institution specified in an EHCP.

- No school or other institution is named in the plan.

- A local authority decides to stop maintaining an EHCP.

- A local authority decides not to amend the EHCP following an annual review.

- A local authority decides not to change the EHCP after carrying out an EHC reassessment.

- Discrimination by a school or local authority in relation to a child or young person's disability.

7.How do I appeal to the tribunal?

The forms that you need to complete are available on the government website. Which form you use will depend upon the reasons for your appeal.

8.What happens after I have submitted my appeal?

Once your appeal has been received by the tribunal service, the following will happen next:

a. The appeal will be registered within 10 working days.

b. The SEND Tribunal let you know that your appeal has now been registered and will provide you with a hearing date.

c. You will be issued with an appeal number – you should use this with all correspondence with the tribunal and the local authority.

d. Case directions, an attendance form and a case management questionnaire are also sent to you.

e. The case directions document states the dates certain tasks must be completed by, some by you (or your representative) and some by the local authority. **You must pay very close attention to these dates!**

f. The case directions will provide a date by which you can submit more evidence.

g. The local authority will receive the same case directions as you, and will then have 30 days to respond. A copy of their response will be sent to you and to the SEND Tribunal.

h. You will be provided with the date, time location of the hearing at least 10 days before it is due to take place.

9.What about the hearing itself?

A hearing at a SEND Tribunal is obviously a legal process, but an attempt is made to try to make it as informal as is possible. This is what will typically happen:

a. The Judge will introduce proceedings, and will outline the issues to be decided during the hearing.

b. Everyone will then be asked to introduce themselves.

c. The Judge will ask you and the other party to provide an opening statement if they wish.

d. Next, the tribunal will go through each issue that needs to be resolved, one at a time.

e. At this point, each party is usually asked to give their opinion and evidence about each of the issues, and to ask questions of the other party.

f. Finally, at the end of the hearing, the Judge will usually ask you (or your representative) and the other party to make any closing statements.

10. When will I hear the outcome?

Under normal circumstances you will hear the decision within 10 working days.

11. How long does the appeals process take?

The whole process, from the point of submitting the application to the actual hearing, takes approximately 5 months. This can vary though depending on the volume of applications.

12. Do I have to pay the tribunal service to make an appeal?

No, there are no court fees involved!

13.Do I have to have legal representation?

At a SEND Tribunal you do not need to have legal representation

Parents may present their own case, pay a representative or, if they wish, instruct a solicitor or barrister.

Not having representation of any kind is obviously the cheapest option, and indeed, I have witnessed parents do this very well. However, due to the emotional attachment involved, as well as the preparation work and the laws and statutory documents that can be involved, some parents pay for representation.

Useful documents and legislation

This is a list of useful documents and legislation that have been referred to in this book, and which you may wish to read from further (all are readily available on line at the time of writing):

1. SEND Code of Practice 2015

2. Children and Families Act 2014

3. United Nations Convention on the Rights of the Child

4. United Nations Convention on the Rights of Persons with Disabilities

5. The Teaching Standards 2011

6. Ensuring a good education for children who cannot attend school because of health needs 2013

7. Supporting pupils at school with medical conditions 2015

8. School attendance 2020

9. Equality Act 2010

10. Equality Act 2010 and Schools 2014

11. SEND Regulations 2014

12. The Education Act 1996.

Quoted Text

- Text within this publication has been quoted from various sources (as they stood as of summer 2021); these sources are identified in the table on the next page.
- The text used is not being used as if it were my own.
- The text has been used in all cases in line with the Open Government Licence(s).
- The owner of the material has not stated that it endorses this publication, and nor is this implied in any way by myself as author of this book.
- Links to the Government Licence(s) are presented at the base of this page.

http://www.nationalarchives.gov.uk/doc/open-government-licence/version/1/

http://www.nationalarchives.gov.uk/doc/open-government-licence/version/3/

http://www.nationalarchives.gov.uk/doc/open-government-licence/version/2

Abbreviation used	Document or legislation	Text used in line with copyright
SCOP	SEND Code of Practice 2015	Open Government Licence v3.0
CFA	Children and Families Act 2014	Open Government Licence v3.0
TS	The Teaching Standards 2011	Open Government Licence v2.0
EAGE	Ensuring a good education for children who cannot attend school because of health needs 2013	Open Government Licence
SCWMC	Supporting pupils at school with medical conditions 2015	Open Government Licence v3.0
SA	School attendance 2020	Open Government Licence v3.0
EA	Equality Act 2010	Open Government Licence v3.0
SENDR	The SEND Regulations 2014	Open Government Licence v3.0
EAAS	Equality Act 2010 and Schools 2014	Open Government Licence v2.0
TEA	The Education Act 1996	Open Government Licence v3.0

About Chris Hadjigeorgiou…

I am an experienced and qualified teacher and SENCo with over 18 years of experience working in schools with children and young people, ranging in age from 3 to 19.

I am now the founder and owner of SEN Achieve, working as an independent Special Educational Needs Adviser supporting parents across the whole of the country. I am also a Registered Test User with the British Psychological Society.

senachieve@outlook.com
www.senachieve.co.uk

SEN Achieve YouTube – Subscribe now!

This is an original publication as written by the author.

Thank you to my children for creating the image on the first page and the two images below.

Printed in Great Britain
by Amazon

13699007R00064